Walk With Me, The Journey

MEMOIRS OF A BROKEN SOUL

Walk With Me, The Journey

MEMOIRS OF A BROKEN SOUL

Published by
LuLu Enterprises, Inc.
3101 Hillsborough Street, Raleigh, NC 27607
www.lulu.com

Cover design by LuLu Enterprises, Inc. & Christopher B. Davis

Cover image by Christopher B. Davis

Printed in the United States of America

DEDICATION

This book is dedicated to all of those who didn't make it out of the *struggle* on this side of life, but wanted to. More importantly, it is dedicated to all of the people who are enduring whatever their *struggle* is now and are looking for a way out. May my life be an inspiration in some way.

To my little cousin Sherman Comegys whom I brought into the "street-life" as a pre-teen and committed suicide at 21 to get away from a life he didn't like, I dedicate this to you. The story, my story, I should've told you, I will now tell the world!

Walk through the mistakes of my life in my pages rather than in life, that way you won't have to go through what I went through.

CONTENTS

From the Beginning...

'80- I was born to 17 year old parents who separated shortly thereafter. I lived with my Moms and I saw my Pops on the weekends and in the summer.

During my early childhood years I grew up all over West Baltimore City, from the inner city to the county. I lived in Lexington Terrace (West Baltimore City's projects), Whitelock and Madison Ave. (the [1]hood), West Coldspring Lane (the hood), Randallstown (the county), and what seemed like everywhere in between.

Moms had two kids by her abusive boyfriend.

In the process of trying to protect my Moms from being beat up one night, my shoulder was dislocated by her boyfriend.

Started having kissing and rubbing sessions during my 4th and 5th grade elementary school years.

After one particular kissing and rubbing session, the girl told her mother and grandmother that I sexually harassed her and they called the police on me.

'91- Moms left me and followed the abusive boyfriend to North Carolina. I started living with my Pops.

By age eleven I progressed *further* into the "street-life" and the "fast-life". I started pursuing sex, porn, masturbating, smoking weed, drinking, engaging in more vandalism and group violence.

I began selling drugs with my cousin.

'94- High-school (Southwestern High—in the hood) kicked off with me and my Pops living with my step-mom and two step-brothers. This was the year I began writing raps. By now I was full-fledge into the "street-life" and "fast-life".

Pops had two kids with my step-mom.

---

[1] "Hood" is a name for rough neighborhoods; in this case they were all in the inner city.

I got kicked out of my first high-school for assaulting one of my teachers.

I worked with my older cousin in an "after-hour-anything-goes" strip club that he partially owned.

'97- Pops and I moved into our own apartment, and I journeyed into a new school (Walbrook High—in the hood).

'98- I was the drug boss of my own two block radius (Walbrook & Ellamont, and Walbrook & Bloomingdale) and the three building apartment community Pops and I lived in. I was a part of the Ellamont Goodfellas clique, which was connected with North and Long Boys.

I signed off and personally stood by and watched a couple of my drug runners rape and beat a woman in the field on the side of my apartment—because she said my crack wasn't all that.

I was the ringleader for a shooting at a car that was posted at our drug strip intersection. The guy identified me to the police as the shooter. I got locked up the week before my high-school graduation. I was eventually bailed out the night before my graduation day. My best friend made sure my school dues were paid and my cap and gown was purchased and fitted. I managed to graduate high-school and walk across the stage.

I was beaten, while unconscious, by a so-called homeboy (another boss) I banged and sold drugs with. I was extremely intoxicated (high and drunk) one night, and as I approached the block we hustled on (Ellamont) I stopped to see the homeboys. The so-called homeboy and I started slap-boxing and wrestling. His pride got hurt because I ended up getting the better of him. When I was walking away, he sucker punched me from behind and then put me in the [2]"L". After a couple of moments everything went black. When I came to, I was bruised and bloody in my bathroom on the phone with my boys on their way to my house. (Know that the story for this specific incident does not end there).

---

[2] The "L" is a headlock that looks like an "L" when applied. It's very deadly, only taking a couple of moments to put a person unconscious.

This is not your typical introduction. What you've read was *snippets* of my first 18 years of life. Like the intro, this book is also in a timeline order. However, the substance of this book was recorded from 1998 to February 2003.

This book is a collaboration of unique writings and narratives about my journey during those several crucial years in my life. With that said, allow me to give a brief, more in-depth summary of my life up to 2003 for the sake of the reader since this is not an autobiography book:

> I was a marine, a hustler, a banger, a convict, an addict, and a whatever else you can think of. By the age of 22, I did more damaging things than most people do in their whole life. I did drugs for 11 years, sold drugs for 7 years until I joined the Marines in 2000, gang banged[3] for 10 years, was addicted to all forms of sex for 10 to 11 years (that includes porn, masturbation, sex with prostitutes, etc), and I ripped and ran *all* over Baltimore City for about 12 years. I've done just about every negative thing a young person can do or think to do— attempted murder, attempted suicide, rape, low level pimping, torture, arson, robbery, vandalism, molestation, and much more. Either I did it firsthand or was a firsthand witness to it. You name it I did it, except for murder (because they got tipped off and got away) and homosexuality.
>
> I've experienced just about every negative thing a young person can experience. I grew up in a broken and abusive home. I was abandoned by my Moms. I was homeless twice as a teenager. I've been locked up in federal, state, and county jail on both coasts. I've been shot at and beat up to the point of unconsciousness and amnesia. And on I can go. I've been involved with the things affiliated with the "street-life" and "fast-life" (e.g. drugs, violence, gangs/cliques, clubbing, party-

---

[3] Gang banging in Baltimore was like gang banging in California but without the color code (ex. red and blue). We didn't call them gangs back in the 90's (like they do presently). We called them cliques designated by neighborhoods, or blocks, and/or drug strips.

ing, [4]wylin', sex, etc). And I've suffered just about all the consequences like flirting with STD's and death, children out of wedlock, abortions, addictions, jail, emotional damage, etc.

So you can see just from this brief summary (and there is more in the details) that I've been there and done that in every facet of life for a young person. This book will take you through a range of my emotions throughout the last 5 years of that life you've just read about. Each individual expression will tell you my journey during those specific years. My highs, my lows, and my in-betweens are within each writing.

This book will allow you a chance to connect with the emotions and expressions most young people experience. For those that may not have these experiences and emotions I hope you take heed to my life and allow it to be a warning for what not to do and how not to live. However, for those that are experiencing these emotions and situations in their life, I hope after reading this book you receive encouragement and a hopeful outlook about your tomorrow. If I can make it out, so can you!

Take the journey, and walk with me.

---

[4] "Wylin" means acting crazy, buck-wild, etc.

~~~~~~~~~~~~~

In spite of everything that I had been through up to this point in my life, 1998 was still one of my pivotal years. During this year my juvenile and adult criminal record was first etched in the books. I graduated from high school, shared an apartment with my Pops in Walbrook Junction (the hood), started college, and turned 18. I thought I was living "the life".

However, it was only the beginning of a journey no one could imagine, not even myself.

"WORLD WAR 4"
Streets of Baltimore

A YO LET ME TELL YOU HOW WE GOT HARM CITY/ BACK IN 1990 WHEN THE STREETS WAS GETTING GRITTY/ WASN'T GRIMEY/ SOCIETY WAS CREEPING ON ME/ CRIME WAS AROUND ME/ LIKE WARS IN THE STREETS OF BALI/ THEN IT WAS FORMED/ THE WORD HARM TIME TO BE BORN/ CHARM WAS NO MORE/ CORRUPTING STREETS WE KNOW AS B-MORE/ THEN THE PROTECTION/ SOON IT WAS IMPLANTED IN OUR BRAINS/ TRE' 8'S AND FOUR 5'S/ YO GLOCKS WAS INSANE/ I REMEMBER WHEN WE USE TO FIST FIGHT IN THE PARKS/ OUT IN THE STREET LIGHTS WHEN IT CAME TIME TO GET DARK/ THEN THE PROTECTION PART/ F@CK THE TALK/ ALL ABOUT THE SPARK/ SEEING LIGHTS IN THE AIR/ (FROM THE GUN)/ NO THE SHARKS/ NI&&AS RUNNING FROM THE NARCS/ WHEN THE SH!T GET THICK/ PLOTTING ALL ABOUT THE STALK/ ON THE SLIM WHO SNITCHED/ FINDING BODY PARTS/ IN SHOPPING CARTS/ IN ALLEYWAYS/ FIEGN CHANTS/ HOWLING LIKE BARKS ON RAINY DAYS/ MURDERS CAME COMMON SURBURBAN AREAS FALLING/ SACRIFICING CHILDREN TO CRACK AND GUNS WHEN BRAWLING/ TRADE BULLETS/ FOR INNOCENT LIVES NOT EVEN CRAWLING/ GOVERNMENT STALLING WHY WE STILL STAND TALL/ SENDING TROOPS/ WE KNOW AS THE O'/ SOMETIMES ONETIME OR THE PO' YO KNOCKERS ON THE LOW/ WORLD WAR 3 BEEN AROUND FOR AWHILE/ THIS A NEW DAY AND TIME JUST LISTEN TO THE RHYMES/ GET READY/ PREPARE FOR WORLD WAR 4/ NEVER THOUGHT/ IT BE ON THE STREETS OF BALTIMORE

HOOK: WORLD WAR 4/ STREETS OF BALTIMORE/ WHAT YOU WANT KID/ NO NEED TO SAY NO MORE

A SON THINK ABOUT IT/ HMMM/ WHERE YOU LIVE AT/ YO REGARDLESS EAST OR WEST NI&&AS ALWAYS STAY STRAPPED/ IF THEY HAD A VEST THEY WEAR IT/ NI&&AS AINT WORRIED/ YOU WE REAL THUGS/ DON'T GIVE A F@CK ABOUT A STEEL STUG/ HATE MUGS/ NI&&AS GET LIT/ JUS' LIKE YOU SMOKE FUGS/ SON WE GOT GUNS LIKE WHATEVER/ IT'S LIKE HARM CITY WAS DRAFTED AND TAUGHT/ STRAIGHT BY THE DEVIL/ GOT

COPS FINDING CATS IN TRUNKS/ DEEP IN THE WATER/ THAT'S HOW WE GOT THE NICKNAME/ HOME OF THE SLAUGHTA/ SLAUGHTA MORE/ MORE NI&&AS IN BALTIMORE/ WE LIVE THIS WAR/ NO SOLDIERS WE WARRIORS/ THE ENDLESS 4/ WORLD TOUR FROM EASTERN SHORE/ BEFORE/ 1990 YOU KNEW THE SCORE/ '98 WAR ONLY PEACE ON THE FLOOR/ A WHORE/ DEFINING OF THAT IS NO MORE/ AINT NO ROOM FOR A BOY/ SINCE AGE 10/ YOU ARE DEPLOYED IN MORTAL COMBAT/ IMMORTAL CONTACT/ A STEEL BAT BEHIND YOUR DOOR THE CORNER WHERE IT LIES AT/ A STEEL BAT TO A STEEL GAT/ WHAT KIND OF SH!T IS THAT/ BILLY CLUBS AIMED FOR YOUR BACK/ THEN THEY CHECK FOR CRACK/ STREETS GETTING CRAZY LIKE BLACK/ WILD LIKE BIG STACKS/ OUT OF CONTROL LIKE FAT SACKS WE STEAL AC'S/ WHEN NIGHTFALLS SUPPOSEDLY DARKNESS/ ALWAYS HARMLESS/ YOU WRONG KID/ IN BALTIMORE THAT'S WHEN WE SPARK SH!T/ NEVER SLEEPING/ HUSTLERS/ SNITCHES ON CREEPING/ THEY LEAKING/ VITAL INFORMATION TO THE DEACON

HOOK

THE STREETS ARE FLOODED/ THE CITY'S OVERPOPULATED/ BALTIMORE IS MARRIED TO DRUGS, GUNS, ITS OVULATED/ PEOPLE ARE INFATUATED WITH THE THOUGHT OF VIOLENCE/ SILENCE/ DON'T DARE COME TO THE TOWN THAT'S WILDEST/ PREDICTIONS/ CONTRADICTING VOICE OF CONTRADICTIONS/ EVICTIONS/ PEOPLE INTERRUPTING OUR PROVISIONS/ IMPOSSIBLE MISSIONS FILLED WITH HOLLOW TIP COLLISIONS/ PLEASE/ BEWARE OF THE CITY OF HARM/ WE AINT WILLIES/ WE TAKE ARMS SWAPPED FOR PHILLIES/ WE SMOKE PHILLIES/ AND GET APPROACHED WITH BLACK BILLIES/ B.C./ D.C./ ONE OF THE ROUGHEST/ JAILS THAT'S TO FULL WITH THE STREETS THAT'S THE TOUGHEST/ FOR THOSE ONES/ WHO GOT CAUGHT UP IN THE RAT/ THE INNOCENT ALWAYS FALL VICTIM TO THE SCRAP/ REMEMBER THAT/ SCARED NI&&AS GET SMACKED/ AND SENT OVER TO WHERE P.C. AT/ YOU AINT NEVER FREE/ WHEN IT COMES TO THE STREETS/ BALTIMORE NI&&AS NEVER FROZE WITH THE HEAT/ NO MATTER WHAT (WHAT!)/ 20 HEADS RAW MEAT/ THE O' COULDN'T STOP US IF THEY HAD THE ARMY/ THEY TRIED IT/ BUT WE STILL COMING OUT THE CLOSET/ BUSSING BACK/ UNTIL WE DIE WE BUSSING GATS/ NI&&AS SCRAPS/ YOU SEE THE NEWS WE COMING BACK/ EVERYDAY MURDERS/

KILLA'S KILLING BURDENS/ FUNERAL HOMES BECOMING DIAGNOSED SURGEONS/ WE URGING/ BUT STILL DON'T KNOW WHAT FOR/ I THANK GOD I SURVIVED THE STREETS OF BALTIMORE

HOOK

1998

~~~~~~~~~~~~~

I hate to say it, but that is the only writing I have before 2000. Every other significant form of expression I wrote before and after this rap for the next 2 years was lost.

From 1998 to the year of the next writing I possess I lived in the apartment with my Pops, went to community college, hung with my boys and the ladies, had sex, got high, rapped, and did the club scene. You know, living "the life". Well, I was living the life so much that I dropped out of college, tried working, pimped a couple of women, and started hustling full-time again (crack and weed). I eventually got evicted. But because I had nowhere else to go I stayed there by myself with no electricity and bounced around from house to house until one of my cousins saw me on my drug strip and offered me a job and a place to stay.

For 6 months in 1999 I was with my cousin working at a bar on Pennsylvania Ave. (Royal Casino), getting high, drinking, clubbing, having sex (from regular women, to junkies, to prostitutes), etc. You know, living "the life" again.

By the end of 1999 I had touched grounds on every hood in West Baltimore City (except for Murphy Homes) for every reason from drugs, to girls, to violence. Living "the life" had me going crazy with no purpose or direction. I found myself jobless, homeless again, and fed up. I needed an outlet outside of being intoxicated and wylin' out.

The day before New Years Eve I went and stayed with my step-mom. While I was there, I realized I had to get away and do something with my life. Otherwise, I'd end up dead or in and out of jail wasting away my life. In came the New Year, I was on my way to the Marine Corps. This is where my latest journey begins, in the new millennium.

"So Beautiful"

You wonder why I stare

Is it the eyes?

Big and brown like Mother Nature

The most beautiful things are among Mother Nature

Your nose and ears fit perfectly like pieces to a puzzle

Lips like cotton candy

Soft, sweet, and pink, sometimes sticky

Though I've never tasted them

Could be addictive, maybe that's why…

Soft to the touch, skin feels like silk

Thoughts of holding her heart, but I can't

When the wind blows I hear her voice, and smell her scent

So beautiful, yet so hard to tell her

If to depict her as a fruit

A peach, ripe and untouched

I can taste her in my sleep

I can taste her when I look into her eyes, even if she's not around

And you wonder why I stare

6/30/00

"So Lovely"

So lovely to the eyes

Your smell is lovely, your touch is lovely, your kiss is lovely

Not love but love..ly

So many names to call you, cuz your face makes me smile

I know a lot of cats want you, cuz you capture their heart with just one smile

Skin so smooth, face so clean

You have natural beauty that's why you're a Queen

I could stare for days at yo beautiful a$$

Such a pleasant view

And you speak, voice so soft it makes my hair stand up

That ain't the only thing that stands up, especially when I see you strut

Words cannot describe how fine you are to me

Damn can I have a kiss?

Mmm, taste how they look

Thank you so much precious for the mind trip we took

7/22/00

~~~~~~~~~~~~~

Those two poems were the start of a relationship that I did not expect. My wife and I met while I was in the service. She was actually my homeboy first. I was too busy trying to get with her homegirls, roommates, and all the other women to notice her. Then, during July of 2000 in Meridian, MS, we took it to another level. As you could see, I was totally into her. However what you don't see is I was still totally into other women as well. Yet, she was the exception because I didn't write the others any poems...not that I can remember. And of course, there's more to that story.

Throughout the time those poems were written I asked my wife to marry me. She said yes and we got married in September of 2000. Yeah, not even 6 months. You could've called it a bittersweet love, because by the end of 2000 (much to my surprise) we were at each other's throats. What a way to bring in the New Year.

2001 was a monumental year for me. My *first* son was born, I dropped my *first* rap album "The Book of Exodus" (in a real recording studio), I was in Cali, and I was turning 21.

I had big plans for 2001.

AUTHORIZED FOR LOCAL REPRODUCTION

MEDICAL RECORD	CHRONOLOGICAL RECORD OF MEDICAL CARE

DATE	SYMPTONS, DIAGNOSIS, TREATMENT, TREATING ORGANIZATION *(Sign each entry)*
9-10-01	NMCP/ MHD.
	Patient evaluated - see prior
	note for full eval
	MSE - No SI/HI +contract
	A - Partner Relational Problem
	Intermittent Explosive D/o
	P - ① F/U 2-3 wks c np
	② Recommend no access
	to weapons. Although
	the patient has not voiced
	SI or HI he has exhibited
	self injurious behavior
	in past under times of
	increased stress

Mary Rusher
LCDR/MC/USN
Psychiatrist

This medical record was reviewed by _____
Chronological order _____ (Yes) _____ (No) _____
Date received _____ Signature _____

HOSPITAL OR MEDICAL FACILITY	STATUS	DEPART./SERVICE	RECORDS MAINTAINED AT
SPONSOR'S NAME	SSN/ID NO.	RELATIONSHIP TO SPONSOR	

PATIENT'S IDENTIFICATION: *(For typed or written entries, give: Name - last, first, middle; ID No or SSN; Sex; Date of Birth; Rank/Grade.)*

	REGISTER NO.	WARD NO.

Davis, C
x 8005

CHRONOLOGICAL RECORD OF MEDICAL CARE
Medical Record
STANDARD FORM 600 (REV. 6-97)
Prescribed by GSA/ICMR
FIRMR (41 CFR) 201-9.202-1

"Psych' Ward"

During the end of 2000 I tried to kill my wife (who was around 4 months pregnant at the time) and myself. I pulled out a butcher's knife and sat on the living room couch and told her, "I dare you try to leave." My wife got away by jumping off the balcony from our second floor apartment. As for me, I set her belongings on fire on the bedroom floor. Then, I sat in the middle of the smoke filled room smoking a Black and Mild while talking to the police on the phone.

For her and my own safety I was arrested and taken to the Balboa Naval Hospital Psychiatric Department. There I was diagnosed with "Intermittent Explosive Disorder". I had to take Depakote and give blood until I was cleared "acceptable on my own" by doctors almost a year later.

In the end, I spent my 20th birthday in the psych' ward. How's that for a birthday present?

That bittersweet love continued.

"Falling Love"

How do you talk to a deaf person?

How do you get a blind person to see you trying?

How do you get a mute to tell you that they're happy?

Can't hurt a wall

But you can hurt a heart built like a wall

To have a pillar of love

Then to break it

To have something as precious as a child

Then to give it away

Why do we hurt those that are innocent?

But yet that's who we love

Does love hurt?

So why hurt the person that loves?

Why not hurt love?

Love is a thing

Love is an idea

Love is something as strong as a pillar, precious as a child, can't hear, see, talk, or move, so innocent, and it can't get hurt

So why hurt the one that you love, when love is such a powerful thing to have?

You hurt more people than you know with love if you misuse it

4/25/01

"SOILED THOUGHTS"

F' ya'll

Everybody got pain

Everybody don't like somebody

Everybody like somebody

What's the difference?

You live to die

So is it a race to die?

Some people say "I want to live forever"

Why?

So you can get tired of living and say "I want this to end"

We all want something out of life

Life wants something from us

Can you guess?

We learn things to understand things

But then we don't want to understand everything

So why waste time learning everything

I love idiots

I hate know-it-alls

Stop trying to know everything

But try and understand *anything*

When you understand anything

Then you'll understand my soiled thoughts

4/25/01

"Marked For Death"

I DONE HAD SLUGS FLY PAST ME/ MIST OF A CROSS FIRE/ I WASN'T EVEN
THE CULPRIT OR A DOPE HIT/ JUST FROM THE WRONG WAY/ IN THE
WRONG PLACE AT THE WRONG TIME/ EVERYTHING WAS WRONG/ EVEN
THE SLUGS CRIED/ AND WHY I/ REMEMBER LISTENING/ I WASN'T
REMINISCING YO BECUZ I HEARD WHISTLING/ BUT NOT FROM THE WIND/
HOW MANY NI&&AS CAN FIT ON THE SIDEWALK/ NOT ENOUGH/ CUZ
THEM BULLETS TOOK A COUPLE IN THE WIND NOW THEY DUST/ RUNNING
FASTER THAN HEART BEATING RACING MYSELF/ PRAYING NOT TO BE THE
NEXT ONE TAKING TO DEATH/ DIPPIN' IN ALLEYS/ DODGING BULLETS AND
NI&&AS/ JUMPING GATES/ AND LEAPING YARDS/ I COULD STILL HERE'EM/
LOOKING BACK I COULD STILL SEE'EM/ THAT WHITE TAURUS 4 NI&&AS
DEEP/ STILL GUNNIN', PACKIN', RELOADIN', AND BLASTING THE HEAT/
DAMN/ YOU THINK THEY WOULD'VE STOP BY NOW/ EVEN IF/ I WANTED
TOO I COULDN'T STOP RIGHT NOW/ LIFE AND DEATH ARE BUT A FEW
STEPS AND SHOTS AWAY/ RUNNING WITHOUT KNOWING IF I'M GOING TO
SEE THE NEXT DAY/ JUST AS STRAYS GRAZE PAST ME/ PINGIN' THE
WALLS/ THINKING IF I WAS HIT/ CUZ I WAS BEGINNING TO FALL/ NOT
KNOWING AT ALL, FACE IN THE CONCRETE/ TOOK A PAUSE/ HEARD A
SCREECH/ THEN I JUMPED TO MY FEET/ JUST THEN, I SEEN THE WHITE
TAURUS ROLLIN' UP THE STREET/ TO MY SURPRISE, THEM NI&&AS
DIDN'T SEE ME/ THEY STILL BLAZIN' MEAN/ THANKING GOD FOR
ALLOWING ME TO SEE SIXTEEN…

LIFE IS LIKE A GAME SON/ WRONG MOVE YOU LOSE/ ONLY DIFFERENCE/
REAL LIVES AND REAL TOOLS/ IT'S A JUNGLE OUTSIDE ONLY THE STRONG
SURVIVE/ AND WHETHER PREY OR PREDATOR IT'S UP TO YOU TO LIVE OR
DIE… THAT'S FOR REAL!

2001

This specific piece was a combination of past events with my vivid imagination to paint the picture. Although I do believe I exaggerated the story for the CD I was doing at the time I wrote it. Nonetheless, it's still a true expression of reality for someone.

"MENTAL DECISIONS"

SCARY FACES/ DISCRIMINATIVE ACTIONS/ CAUSE FOR ME TO BLAST IN/ POLITICIANS BACK IN/ ANTI-TRUST/ TRUE LIES GOT TOO MUCH/ QUOTE "THE TRUTH WILL NEVER LIE IN THIS DAY GOD WE TRUST"/ BE MODEST PLEASE THE WORLD YOU SEE IS AN ODYSSEY/ AND WE'RE RAN BY A TYRANNY ANARCHY/ STOP THE PRESS/ 9-1-1 WAS A TEST/ NOW REVERT BACK TO HOOD MENTALITY/ HOOD BRUTALITY/ SCOTCH TAPE OVER WOUNDS/ SALT SLUGS IN YA FOOD/ INSTRUMENTS ARE USED TO PLAY PARTS TO SOUND UP THE DARK/ SPARK UP ON YA INTEREST/ MIND MADE'N GUNS PERSUADING/ COP KILLINGS THROUGH AGES A CHAPTER IN THE HISTORY PAGES/ BODY HARVEST SEPARATES THE WEAK FROM THE HARDEST/ YOU KNOW I GOT THAT PROBLEM SOLVER MIND REVOLVER/ LEAVING SMOKE FUMES FLOODING LIKE CRACK ROOMS/ THE OPIUM BLOOMS/ SADASTICAL PHYSICAL PUNISHMENT OF THE MIND/ I SPECIALIZE IN CONTROLLING SUICIDAL THOUGHTS/ BUT USE HAND TO HAND ENCOUNTERS FOR NI&&AS BODIES I TOSSED/ BODIES IS LOST/ MISSING PERSON REPORTS/ THOUSAND IS DEAD/ THOUSANDS OF THEM IN COURT/ WHO SORT/ SOME TAUGHT SOME FOUGHT/ THAT'S WHY I SAID IT'S A BLOOD SPORT/ A BLOOD SPORT/ GET IT/ BLOOD SPORT...

After 9/11, 2001

"UNTOLD STORIES"

I AWAIT/ FOR THIS CAT/ TO PLACE HIS FATE, IN THE/ PALM OF MY HANDS/ YO HE USE TO BE MY MAN/ I DIDN'T UNDERSTAND WHY/ BUT I'MA APPREHEND MY BALLS BACK/ CUZ I'MA TAKE'M STRAIGHT FROM HIS NUT SACK/ HERE WE GO/ NOW IT'S TIME FOR THE MAIN SHOW/ ENTER THE HOUSE THROUGH THE BACK BASEMENT WINDOW/ CREEPING IN REAL SLOW/ NO NOISE HE'LL NEVER KNOW/ QUIET AS KEPT/ AS I CREPT UP THE STEPS/ I HERE THE RADIO PLAYING/ PERFECT DISTRACTION/ ANYTHING FAILS I BROUGHT THE SNUB JUST TO BLAST HIM/ I HIT THE LIGHT SWITCH/ TO KEEP THE DARK SENSE/ FROM THE BASEMENT TO THE HALLWAY TO THE KITCHEN/ I GRABBED A STEAK KNIFE/ HOPING HE COMPLETED EVERYTHING HE WANTED TO IN THE 20 YEARS OF HIS LIFE/ GETTING CLOSER/ TO THE RADIO SOUND/ AND MY MIND STARTS REPLAYING FROM THAT FRIDAY DOWNTOWN/ 5 ROUNDS/ I DON'T WANNA BLAST'EM/ I WANNA GUT'EM/ LET'EM DIE SLOW, FROM HIS OWN BLOOD CHOKING AND STRUGGLING/ THEN I HEARD A COCK/ STOP/ WAS I KNOWN/ DID THIS/ NI&&A KNOW THAT I WAS UP IN HIS HOME/ F@CK IT/ THE MISSION'S STILL ON/ NOW I'M AT THE DOOR WHERE HE REST HIS HEAD AT/ IT'S TIME TO DEAD THAT/ I SEE'EM WALKING/ THROUGH THE CRACK OF THE DOOR/ I HERE'EM TALKING, AND I KNOW HE'LL SCREAM JUST LIKE A WHORE/ THE SCORE/ HE GOT HIS BACK TURNED/ ENTERED THE ROOM FAST/ THROUGH HIM IN THE L' THE MORE STRUGGLE MORE BREATH BURNED/ WHISPERED IN HIS EAR/ "WAS MY WIFE WORTH YA LIFE B!TCH"/ THAT SAME MOMENT STEAK KNIFE TO HIS THROAT QUICK/ TOOK HIS BODY IN THE BEDROOMS BATHROOM/ PUT'EM IN THE TUB WITH THE SHOWER RUNNING BLOOD POOL/ TOOK THE KNIFE WIPED IT OFF PUT IS IN HIS HAND/ SUICIDE NOTE/ ON THE COUNTER SIGNED WITH A BLOODY STAMP

HOOK: IN THE WIND YOU HEAR WHISPERS OF MEN/ BEGGING FOR LIFE/ PAYING FOR DEATH AT A FULL PRICE

ON THE OTHER SIDE OF TOWN/ THIS CHICK I USE TO GET DOWN WITH/ CLAIM SHE LOVES ME/ AND F@CK ANOTHER NI&&A D!CK/ THAT TYPE OF SH!T MAKES ME SICK/ I HAD A SEED BY HER/ SO I CALLED MY MAN J HE A

WIFE BEATER/ ALL HE ROCK IS WIFE BEATERS/ I TOLD HIM THE SCOOP/ HE
SAID, (YO I GOTTA MEET HER)/ BETTER YET, WHEN YOU GREET HER SON/
DO IT RIGHT HOLLA AT HER/ AND TRY YA BEST YO/ TO TAKE HER HOME
THAT SAME NIGHT/ THE NEXT NIGHT J HIT ME ON THE CELL/ (A YO I'M AT
THE B!TCH CRIB)/ WORD NI&&A WHAT'S THE DEAL/ (IT'S JUST US 2)/ (I
DON'T SEE YA SEED)/ GOOD MONEY CLOSE THE BLINDS ON THE BALCONY/
(A YO, HERE SHE COME I HIT YOU BACK LATER ONE)/ NOW I'M/ BLOWING
A DUTCH THINKING TO MYSELF WHAT'S UP/ DID HE DEAD HER/ OR HE IS
JUST DIGGING IN HER GUTS/ MAN F@CK IT/ NOW I'M DIALING TEN DIGITS/
HE PICKS IT UP ON THE 1ST RING AND HOLLAS (WHO IS IT)/ YO WHAT YOU
DOING NI&&A/ (I GOT HER WRAPPED UP IN THE TRASH BAG 'BOUT TO
DUMP HER BODY IN THE RIVER)/ WORD SO HOW YOU DO IT/ (NOT OVER
THE CELLY)/ (BUT I HIT YOU UP IN MINUTE YO AND THEN I'LL TELL YOU)/
JUST THEN I REMEMBER HER LITTLE SECRET/ SHE HATES DARK PLACES,
SO SHE CLOSE HER EYES/ THEN SHE STOPS HERSELF FROM BREATHING/ J
HIT ME UP LATER/ TOLD ME THAT HE USED PLASTIC WRAP/ WRAPPED HER
FACE AND LEFT HER ON THE TOILET PEEING/ THEN HE SMOKED A BLUNT
IN THE ROOM TO MELLOW OUT/ CAME BACK AND BAGGED HER BODY AND
THE REST IS FLOATING DOWN STREAM

HOOK: IN THE WIND YOU HEAR ECHOES OF CRIES/ SCREAMING TELL ME
WHY/ I LOVE YOU SO MUCH THAT I RATHER DIE

11/6/2001

During the specific time I wrote this piece my wife and I were separated. I
stayed in the Marine barracks, while my wife and my son lived in [5]base-
housing.

One night in the early part of November, I watched my son while my
wife, her girlfriend, and two of my homeboys went to the club. The
homeboy spoken of in this song was supposed to be getting with my

---

[5] "Base housing" is a house provided by the Marines on base.

wife's girlfriend. However he didn't just flirt with her, he flirted with my wife also at the club. Grimy right?

It gets worse.

Later that night, after I went back to my barracks room, my wife let the "grimy homeboy" lay in the bed with her and her girlfriend. Sounds and smells fishy don't it? My other homeboy (the real friend) only went with them and stayed over simply to watch out for my wife and make sure nothing happened. He thought the grimy homeboy was scheming. Well, he fell asleep before the others. He never knew what was going on.

The next day I went to my wife's house, and I don't remember how, but in came drama. In the midst of the commotion, my wife screams out in anger, "that's why I f@cked ya boy last night." I completely lost it. I went to my trunk, grabbed the crowbar, and went straight after her. My real homeboy tried his best to stop me, and ended up telling me, while holding my son in his car seat, to think of my son. So I turned around and I went and smashed *all* of the windows on her brand new, not even a month owned, 2001 pearl white Sonata with the crowbar. Then I walked away smoking a Black and Mild. The Military police eventually came and arrested me. After I got released, I wrote this song to vent.

On another note, I really tried to kill the grimy homeboy too. But, people we were mutually close with kept me from doing it. One night during a barracks wide blackout, I dressed in my inside out navy blue sweats with a black skull cap, had my homemade [6]shank, and went up to his barracks room. As I approached his room, another friend of ours saw me and knew what I had in mind. He pulled me in another marine's room and they talked me out of it.

---

[6] A "shank" is a makeshift knife or dagger.

"SHADY GUYS"

I HATE SHADY GUYS/ RUNNY MOUTHS WITH MY SHINE IN THEY EYES/ WHO SEEK MY DEMISE/ DESPISED/ I'M A DIE TO GET MINE/ I'M GUNNIN' YOU BLIND/ YA KIND IS THE KIND THAT TOOK MY KINDNESS FOR WEAKNESS/ NOW I'M 'BOUT TO SPARK THEM HEATERS/ LEAVE YA RUNNY MOUTH SPEECHLESS/ BODY BREATHLESS/ STRESS ELEVATED/ EASILY STATED/ YOU TWO FACE'ED/ WANTED DECAPITATED FROM YA MIND BODY AND SOUL/ MY HEART IS TOO COLD/ YOU CROSS THAT LINE NOW YA END HAS BEEN SOLD/ I PLAY TO YOU FOLD/ BOLD/ YOU DISRESPECTING MY FAMM/ YOU TESTING MY MANHOOD/ NOW YA A$$ IN A JAM/ UNDERSTAND/ I BET YA LIFE THAT MY GUN IT WON'T JAM/ UNDERSTAND/ I AINT PLAYING NO MORE/ I'M LAYING YOU WHORES/ WHOLE FAMILY AT THE CHURCH ALTAR PRAYING TO THE LORD

12/19/2001

I wrote this song after I came back and heard that the marine I rapped with in Cali was trying to get with my wife repeatedly while I was gone on leave[7] in Baltimore.

---

[7] "Leave" is the term used in the Marines for vacation.

As you can see, 2001 was a year of dramatic changes. That's not including my son being born in July, then me leaving him and my wife to go back to Baltimore a week after his birth. What a way to start fatherhood. But the changes don't stop there.

In 2002 I went from having a car, money, doing a compilation album, my songs being played in clubs, and clubbing (from Tijuana, Mex. to Riverside, Ca.), to possibly divorcing my wife, my demo being rejected by Capitol Records (or so I thought—after I got locked up the agent used my demo songs for his Mexican rap group who got signed and my songs were played on the radio), losing money for getting into trouble with the military, being put on restriction[8] *multiple* times, going UA (unauthorized absence) for 29 days, and then getting kicked out the Marines altogether. Talk about changes. This all happened within a matter of months!

Get ready for a long stretch that continues with more theatrical changes. Actually, the changes take a deeper look into the mind and heart of a young adult with no other outlet but paper (or a keyboard), drugs, and alcohol.

This book doesn't only reveal what was going on in *my* mind and *my* heart. It's probably what goes through the minds and hearts of *most* teens and young adults at some point in their young life.

---

[8] "Restriction" is the Marines version of house arrest.

"Hate Me"

You can hate me for life/

I don't care I'ma still be trife/

Can use a knife but choose my gun and my fist/

I'm loading clips or loading knuckles to ya lips/

We can play games/

Gun roulette at face range/

F@ck a beef/

I gotta grave for every enemy/

I'm murder finicky/

You like to sing a lot/

I make my slugs be ya symphony/

I gotta tendency/

Quick to blast a ni&&a/

Quick to stash a ni&&a/

No remorse to catch my feelings you betta flash the picture

2002

"CRIME SENSE"

CONFRONTATIONS OF THE RIGHT KIND/

IS WHY A NI&&A KEEP HIS HAND GRIPPED ON THAT NINE/

SUBLIME PUNISHMENT/

GUN GRIP YA WIFE CLIT/

F@CK THE BULLSH!T/

YOU KNOW WE GOT THEM OTHER CLIPS/

READY FOR WAR SH!T/

UNLOADING BANK VAULTS/

NO GLOVES, FINGERPRINTS BROWN FROM BLUNTS SPARKED/

I LEAVE A STICKY TRAIL/

FOLLOW MEEEEE!

TO WHERE THE SLUGS RAIN LIKE HAIL/

HELL IS ON EARTH/

THAT WHY THIS LIFE IS DEEP IN THE DIRT/

GET F@CKED IF YOU FLIRT/

THAT'S WHY THEY SAY THAT DEATH'S IN A SKIRT/

YOU LOVE WHO YOU HURT/

AND HURT WHO YOU LOVE/

THAT'S WHY WE SCREAM WE LOVE OUR LIFE, CUZ IT HURTS WHEN WE STRUGGLE/

FORCED INTO TUSSLES/

LEARNED HOW TO USE THEM FORCE IN OUR MUSCLES/

KNOWING THAT DEATH IS NEAR WHEN YOU HEAR THE VIOLENCE IS MUFFLED...

(A YO, A YO, A YO,

WHAT YOU DOING YO, WHAT YOU DOING YO

BLAH, BLAH, BLAH)

HOOK: CRIME SENSE/

     IT'S A THUG AND HUSTLA'S MENTALITY/

     CRIME SENSE/

     IT'S THE DRUG TO FAKE NI&&A'S FATALITIES/

     CRIME SENSE/

     IT'S THE INSTINCT ON HOW TO SURVIVE/

     CRIME SENSE/

     IT'S THE REASON NI&&A'S LIVE TO DIE

2002

"Let It Flow"

I speak to the world on a level only few are on

So you catch up, not me slow down!

Elevate yo mind young man, old man, young women, old women

Speak yo heart, let the mind wander plains unknown to man

Knowledge is contagious

A mind is a powerful thing to waste

So why waste it

Educate yo'self people

Ditto, as I need too

Are you ready for mental warfare?

Don't strap up with book smarts

You are a weapon, learn yo'self

Stop trying to learn everybody else

Time wasted was preciousness not cherished

Average life span is what?

When God says it's time, that's when

So 'til then, live life don't let life live you

Words from a broken man putting himself back together by hand

I am

Whateva I want to be

Feel me!

7/22/2002

"Words From The Heart"

I ride in silence (pause)

I let my heart speak, cuz my mind is sleep

Finally peace

Ooohhh, why more drama?

Can I just rest in peace, or do I have to wait until I rest in peace?

My heart speaks cuz my mind is sleep

Hunger pains and thirst for knowledge

I took a year in college but that's not the knowledge I'm talking about

Power

Self control over self control from self control to gain self control

My heart speaks cuz my mind is sleep

So many questions

Doubts to fears, no just live!

I ride in silence

I let my heart speak, cuz my mind is sleep

Finally peace

7/22/2002

"MIXTURE"

So much anger inside

Boxed in for years

Unwanted tears cuz I lived in fear

Unheard cries at night screaming come home

To wake up to see that I was alone

Grow some balls suck it up you'll see

That my strength came from hardworking in poverty

Yet as a young adolescence, my focus turned street

Street is as street does, so I sleep wit no peace

Dreams of death, dreams of life

But what purpose?

Dreamt of breath for my wife

I never thought

I gotta seed created from love

Yet love is an action

Me knowing it was a blessing from above

But love was the action

Why am I more scared now than I was before?

What does gravity or nature taken its course have to do with glory?

The words "close your eyes and pray child" echo in my head

But when I close my eyes

I feel nothing, silence, I'm dead

7/22/2002

"A Talk With A Psychiatrist"

Why me Lord?

My little frame can carry half the world's weight on my shoulders

That's a question

My mind able to subdue so much stress

Aren't we all chosen?

Or am I chosen for just pain and agony?

The love of my life is my son

And you blessed me with him, so you should be the love of my life

You are, but why does it not feel the same as my son?

Is my hardships and trials due because I do not love you as I love my son?

Maybe I've just answered my own questions

Or am I 'noid?

Yet paranoia is the state of being aware

So if I'm aware of my problem, then I should be able to solve it, correct?

Questions with answers that only One person knows

Why me Lord?

Am I the only person who thinks this way?

(Snap) Wake up, recognize, and realize, that this is reality

Damn, why me Lord?

7/22/2002

All of the poems that were written on 7/22/02 were motivated by a book I was reading at that time and a cross-country bus trip I was on. This took place during my return back from being UA 26 days in Baltimore. I spent the next 3 days UA in California before I turned myself in.

"ANGRY LITTLE MAN"

Souls torn between heaven and hell

Anger festers, blood boils, ice grilling whateva

F@ck'em all! For real for real!

Give me something or don't give me sh!t

If I'm determined, then you're dead regardless

Big cold heartless sponsor for death

Stop trembling, I can't think straight

Hot tears roll down my face, blurry vision, still wylin

Innocent bystanders caught in a thug's mission

A funeral is the best way to meet people

They say, "you greet people dead or alive, but you learn about deceased people"

Acknowledge another day

If you ain't famm and you caught with a stare you dead where you fear

If you ain't my famm, that's a hint, so you better beware

If wisdom is the capacity... Then my mind is blasphemy...
But my soul is anointed by the one who appointed me to be wise

2002

"Trapped"

Set me free

Why does a man cry?

Cuz something is trapped

Love, pain, anger, emotions building but can't...

Let it go

Smiley faces and laughter hides the real man trapped inside

Be patient!

God's soft voice continues to echo, but anger continues to boil

They say the grass is greener on the other side

Not always

Happiness trapped, inner child caged in due to the surroundings of one's environment

F@ck that!

I will not be a slave to my own self

I broke the chains when I entered this world

Yet they're still there

Trapped

No matter wherever whenever

Trapped

Until your soul's set free

Trapped

Naw ni&&a not me

Trapped

7/30/02

"THE TRUTH"

Shiddd I don't know sh!t

Love to learn, and want to apply it

What's my talents, my goals, my dreams, my frustrations?

Got a whole lot of negativity inside

Multiple personalities causes my headaches

Loved once and turned it down

Created love out of love and still don't know how to love

Damn I talk too much!

What's my purpose here?

My life is worth what?

How many of ya'll love me, truly?

I speak the truth bluntly, and lie through deception

F@ck how you feel, I read books, smoke weed, rap, cuss, fuss, fight, whine, complain, and I'm too damn sexy!

But what does all this mean?

Thoughts of wisdom, false knowledge, frontin' like I know

Where is my life going? Up in smoke, down the toilet, with the birds, or in the clouds?

Shiddd I don't know…

Am I lost?

No!

I'm right here, but I don't know where, or what, or when, or how

And that's the truth, I don't know sh!t

Bullsh!t!

I'm a real a$$ ni&&a, who's a father to his son, in control of his life, got his dignity, and self-respect

The truth is, I know what I want and what I can settle for

My mind is too powerful to let negativity over run me

That's me!

Determined, strong-willed, hard-headed, and stubborn

That's me!

Respectful, gentlemen like, but thugged out

That's me!

A hee-me head[9], with the mind capacity of Einstein

That's me!

Who don't give a f@ck, but cautious at times

That's me!

Witty, clever, gifted, and family oriented

That's me!

---

[9] A "hee-me head" was a term used by one hip-hop artist, it means a serious pothead.

Like me or leave me

And that's the truth

But I don't know sh!t, right!

Riiiggghhhttt!

What's your truth is the question

Don't judge me, judge yo'self

And that's the truth

8/7/02

"Am I"

Why am I here?

What's my purpose?

They say I'm creative but no direction

I'm urgent with no priority

That don't make sense

Am I here for a reason, or just a body taken up space?

My son loves me

Is that why I'm here?

But I gave him back to the One who gave him to me

So again, what's my purpose?

Am I a voice for people?

Or am I a noise that just aggravates people?

Do I make any sense?

Am I a temper waiting to blow on any and everybody?

Probably!

My luck, I'm another body to help fill up a prison or a grave

I'm just a statistic!

I will not be known as a b!tch or a failure, since I'm wanted dead or alive by myself

Am I crazy?

You come walk in my shoes and then you tell me am I… crazy

Am I tired?

You damn right! Tired of repetitive bullsh!t

My life is that which I speak

Now I lay me down to sleep, I pray my Lord my soul you keep. Give me peace so do not wake...me up to see another day.

Am I dead yet?

8/16/02

"Am I" was the poem I wrote once it registered that I was about to get kicked out of the Marines. That's when I began to realize I've never completed anything in my life. I was a total failure, so what was the purpose of living.

"ANGRY LOVE"

I say, "it's better not to love, than to love at all"

It's funny, the one that knows you the best is the one that hurts you the most

What's love?

Love is what you do, not how you feel

So is hurting the one you claim you love, love?

Since it's what you do, not how you feel

Thoughts and visions of endless pain

Make you scream, and I'm not talking about my name

I want you to feel how I feel when you get me heated!

Calling you names

21 years old and still playing games

Who's childish?

Me, cuz you my first

Or you, cuz your first played you worst and you just taken it out on me

Questions you've answered before, but your actions tell me different

Actions speak louder than words

Words hurt, but actions kill

I'm not perfect: cheating, flirting, taunting, cursing

My flaws I do not hide

You get what you see

I see you, but I don't see you

So who hiding, or frontin' real good?

God made man and then woman so the man wouldn't be alone

Well because of you, I only have one thing to say

I choose to be alone! Don't bother, I know my way home

Now what love gotta do with that?

8/19/02

"FREESTYLE POETRY"

Voices…

Soft, loud, shook, faint, scared, deep

All different personalities

Am I selfish, cuz I only worry about me?

F@ck you, you, and you

That's me

Cries…

Screams, panting, moaning, whining, sniffling, suffocating

Stop hesitating, pull it!

Your life or mine, pull it!!

Death is life

Feel that, that's some deep sh!t

You live to die, so die to live

It ain't hard, either you here or you not

I could give a f@ck

I'm here to you pull it!

Sh1t!

Gimmie some weed, let me smoke my brain housing…

Went blank

Body aching for the touch

Anxious to leave

What I got, same thing over there

Sh1t!

Denying any form of positive entry in my mind

Laughter wins it all

Hate takes the victory

Life suffers

Death conquers, while crowning the king

And my spirit is set free

That I am… free!

8/19/02

"Honestly…"

Honestly…

Play chess more ways than one/

More bodies to dump/

More hobbies for fun/

More hollows for guns/

Still shadow the slums/

Politicking my duns, my sons first on this earth/

Sworn at his birth/ that I would be his father 'til I'm put in a hearse/

Honestly…

Minutes are worth gold/ times as priceless as platinum sold/

Double ya role/

Then triple ice on a cold heart/

From the start/ smoking, rapping, killing, with my life for this world I fought/

Honestly…

I get high like Vietnam/ I see death like the Vietcong/

Better be warned, in the city of harm/

And get out the way when them pistols is drawn/

HONESTLY...

FULLY ARMED GUARDS, AND THAT'S JUST TO ENTER THE 'JETS/ (PROJECTS)

SO IMAGINE HIGH PRICE FACILITIES, LASER BEAMS BE DOING ALL OF THE CHECKS/

HONESTLY...

THAT'S THE WORLD AFTER 9-1-1/

BUT 9-1-1 HAS BEEN HAPPENING ON THE STREETS WHERE I'M FROM

8/22/02

"Fear"

You can see it in someone's eyes

You can feel it when they walk past

It ain't the size of the man, it's the determination of the man

"Stop eyeballing me"

Why?

Afraid I'm gonna find out your little secret

Scared a$$ grown man!

I'm a buck fifty!

F@ck you scared of!

My eyes cry pain and anger

My words say passion and hate

Sh!t I'm scared of myself, when my temper flares

Eyes stare, you scared,

You dare, you dead

Talk to much

Cool!

I shut up, be warned though

To unpredictable

So what you gonna do now?

"I gave you fair warning, beware!"

8/29/02

August of 2002 was a very interesting month. I was in the process of being kicked out the Marines, I was on restriction again, and I was being considered for either the Brig (military jail) or CCU (correctional custody unit).

Right before I went UA I read up on the crime I was getting ready to commit. I knew there was no Brig time involved, but CCU was an option of punishment. I also read up on the number of NJP's (non-judicial punishment) a marine can receive before being discharged. I had already superseded the amount (which was two), and was working on my fourth.

With all this information in mind, I proceeded to "request mast"[10] to the Lt. General of something like the Marine Division in the Pacific Region. I wanted to rattle my superiors' cages and let them know I am not your typical "urban jarhead". I know more than I let on to. This was all a part of a plan to get a better discharge and released sooner, rather than a Bad Conduct Discharge (equivalent to a felony), Brig time, and a long delay in being released.

This poem was written after I sent my request mast and a fax to the Senator about the military's conduct towards their marines. My superiors didn't look too kindly at me during that time. My wife and the other marines I knew use to say, "You got the whole Command [11]shook."

---

[10] "Request mast" is requesting to speak to a superior on behalf of a serious situation.
[11] "Shook" in this context is a slang term for scared, frightened, nervous, etc.

"Inside Of My Brain"

I came to bring my pain/ go inside of my brain/ and I'll show why I rhyme in vein

I live hard/

I fight hard/

I rap hard/

I pray to God my skills a lil to far/

For anybody to grasp, can't imitate me/

Live my life, walk my shoes, still wanna be me/

Go through my trials and tribulations/

Still I'm formulating, on making my life successful/

By defeating Satan/

God I'm waiting/

Lord call me please!!!/

I gave my son to you, on the day he was conceived/

And still I bleed/

Blue blood, steel slugs/

Are you ready for me/

F@ck love, grave dug/

Can't stop the pain from calling/

ANGERS BRAWLING/

YET I WANT PEACE IN MY LIFE/

BUT I'M FALLING/

FOR REAL LORD WHAT'S THE MATTER/

SHOULD OF MADE ME BLACKER/

SO I HAD A CULTURE TO BLEND IN INSTEAD OF LAUGHTER/

BEFORE AND AFTER/

I'M STILL SH!T GOD WHY/

TROUBLE CONSTANTLY FOLLOWING ME, STEADILY I PRAY THAT I DIE/

IT'S MY LIFE OR THEIRS LORD/

I'M NOT A JUDGER BUT A TAKER/

'94 I WOULDA TOOK A COUPLE OF THEM HATA'S/

DEATH STEADY HAUNTS ME/

JAIL CELLS TAUNT ME/

I TOLD YOU THE TRUTH, SO FINALLY SET MY SOUL FREE

2002

"I Ain't Shhh"

Due to my Other Than Honorable discharge from the military, my chances of getting a good job or a job period is 20 out of 100.

Do I give up? Naw that's not me. Do I just stop and let nature be? Am I going to be another ni&&a with no job?

I f@cked up every chance I had. Sh!t maybe it's what's meant to be.

- No education

- Pothead

- Quick temper

- Impatient

Typical ni&&a right! No experience. Willing to learn, but who wants to teach. No trades, gifts, talents, or skills, but talking a good game.

That will get me sh1t!

The only way I'm going to make something of myself is to get a degree, or get famous. Both seem inevitable.

Maybe I'm just fooling myself

I ain't sh!t right... riigghht!

2002

"LOOK HOW IT GOT ME"

Weed has affected me in these ways:

- Bad memory

- Broke d!ck

- Loss of weight

- Loss of aspirations, dreams, and goals once set forth by me

- Not following through with things

- Bad eyesight

- 10 years of my life with nothing to show

- Near death experiences

- Displacement from reality and fantasy

- Bad nerves

- Loss of appetite

- Easily irritated

I had to leave Satan alone one day; you'll come to realize that *it's* not helping you, but hurting you.

I understand I have problems. Then I realized that I caused some of my problems by smoking green as long as I have been.

2002

"MY STRUGGLES"

I love to struggle

Makes you strong

I love life

Life is hard

But it makes you strong

Breakdown to rebuild

Outside cries

Inside screams

War is a conquest, but when conquered what have you gained

I was born in a war

Struggled in a war

Loved in a war

My life is a constant war

When I make it successfully (you know, conquering war)

What have I truly gained?

Lost friends

Lost love

Lost thoughts

I don't know no more!

The everyday struggle of a man without…

No one to relate with…

My Child Will Not Struggle!!!

So many tears

No one knows why?

Why me man!

Ever screamed and no one heard it

Ever screamed so loud you knew the world heard, but no one heard it

Even my raps is whack

The talent I thought I had I don't

Wasn't born with a gift, don't have a talent

Yeah, I'm just a body in the world's population

Must've smoked too many knowledge bones

No one to blame but myself

Shiddd, my world…

My struggles

What I do now?

Remember, I love to struggle

I guess that's my gift

What a gift

11/14/02

"Jus Venting"

Take a journey real quick

My minds sick, split personality syndrome

I lost home at 16 years old

Rap feign like nicotine, smoke all day

Rap in my veins, raps on my brain, all day

Besides my son, money, and sex

I vent when I write, vent about my life

Love only had once

And yo' I hated a bunch

And yet I'm still here

Still fighting the fear

Here hands tied, eyes close, pen to the pad

Ill flow, written style yo', I'm letting ya'll know

I don't freestyle well

But I scrap well, rock bells like L', and eluding the cells,

Still polluting the wells, screw a wish, the struggles will tell

What a man's been through

It's like constantly fighting the flu

BODY CAN'T PRODUCE, MIND CAN'T CONTROL, HEARTS TO COLD

I'M NOT OLD

IT'S NOT OVER YET

I CAN STILL BE A SOBER VET'

STRONG IN MY WAYS, I SEE MY SON IN MY FACE

THE MIRROR REFLECTED HIS FUTURE SON I'M SEEING MY FACE

JUS' FINISHED BEATING MY CASE

YET I'M STILL COMPETING MY RACE

COMPLETING MY FATE

ONLY GOD CAN SAVE

BORN BRAVE IN THIS WORLD

1ST CHILD TO MY MOTHER AND FATHER

LIVE IN A TOWN WHERE 25% OR MORE GETS SLAUGHTERED

SO DON'T BOTHER

ASKING ME MY PROBLEM

WHAT THE F@CK IS YOURS

I PLAY THE CARDS THAT I'M DEALT

I'M TRY AN HELP

I TRY TO GIVE AS MUCH AS I CAN

I TRY TO BE A HAPPY MAN

FATHER FORGIVE, I TRY TO UNDERSTAND

BUT SCREW THE WORLD'S PROBLEMS

I GOTTA LIFE TO LIVE

I GOTTA SON TO FEED, AND AIR TO BREATHE, AND VERSES TO READ, AND BLOOD TO BLEED, AND STILL I PLEAD,

PLEASE

FATHER, HELP ME

HOOK: JUS' VENTING FROM A PERSPECTIVE OF NI&&AS IN THE STRUGGLE/

I'M HERE TO HELP YA'LL OUT/

AND IF MY VENTING IS HELPING NI&&AS ON TOP, IN THEY OWN STRUGGLE/

I'M GLAD TO HELP YA'LL OUT/

11/18/2002

"Inside The Mind Of A Madman"

Inside the mind of a madman

I still got pain

My brain is straining from constantly thinking on what to do next

I can't cash a tech

I can't blaze a check

I'm vexed

Wylin' out on corner stores

I played games wit' ni&&as heads at squadron tours

At air stations on the Cali shores

Under the cars of fake wanna-be superstars

Losing God

Eyes bloodshot red

Setting, plotting, contemplating on another ni&&as bread

Fed's and dred's is like weed and cops

Feed the block wit more feigns and rocks

Don't plead the stop

I need the rock

I gotta vent the rest

I STILL GOT PAIN AND AGONY UNLEASHED IN MY CHEST

FORCED TO PRESS ON

MY SONS A BLESSING STILL I'M LIVING

HUNGRY, STRIVING, READY FOR A KILLING THIS IS HOW I'M FEELING

YEAH, THIS IS HOW I'M FEELING

HOOK: INSIDE THE MIND OF A MADMAN…

(CHOP) IT'S KINDA SCARY EERIE THINKING…

(CHOP) I STILL GOT PAIN, MY BRAIN IS STRAIN…

(CHOP) MY INNERS GROWLING FOR SOMETHING TO FEED ON…

(CHOP) CAN'T CASH A TECH, BLAZE A CHECK, I'M VEXED!

INSIDE THE MIND OF A MADMAN

MY INNERS GROWLING

HUNGRY AND THIRSTY FOR SOMETHING TO FEED ON

I NEED HONESTY

REALITY IS JUST A SHADOW IMAGE OF DEPRESSION

I'M RESTING MY SMITH AND WESSON TO GET MY MENTAL ERECTION

BUSS OFF TWICE

THE BUZZ-SAW'S NICE

THE BUCKSHOT'S RIGHT

THE RIPTIDE IS OUT TONIGHT

MY MIND'S A RIP CURRENT FOR THE SAKE OF MY ENEMIES

RIDING THE BREEZE, GET BODIED YOU BREATHE, DON'T DOUBT IT YOU'LL SEE

CAREER PATH IN LARCENY

I EVEN OFF THE -----DENT IF THE OFFERS SPEAK

ROBBING LEACHES

I WANT ALL, EVEN THE BLOOD

F@CK DOGS AND THUGS, MUGS AND SLUGS

I'M THE GRIM REAPER, JUST OFF THE ONE YOU LOVE

I'M THE GRIM REAPER, JUST OFF THE ONE YOU LOVE

HOOK

INSIDE THE MIND OF A MADMAN

IT'S KINDA SCARY EERIE THINKING

WHEN HE GETS QUIET, STRATEGE PLANNING

ON THE NEXT MAN HE'S APPREHENDING

PRIOR PLANNING FOR THE KILLING GOT FIG'A WHICH WEAPON

WIRE TO CHOKE

GUN TO GUT

KNIFE TO THROAT

WHICHEVER HE CHOOSE, SUN LOW YOU GO

No shots ringing

Only fire bringing from the pits of hell

And his warriors as well

Ready for war

Death conquers all

One day we fall

We all praise some god

Even homicidal maniacs

And suicidal looney-cats

Use some fire, burn his sh!t

Get a knife then stab his chick

Get his peoples fat a$$ and he stuffing this pig

Ni&&as f@cking his wiz

Running his kids

What kinda life is this?

What kinda life is this!

Hook

11/18/2002

"Masterpiece"

Thanks to the anointed one who appointed me wise

[12]C.O.D.E the disguise ya'll guys can't afford it

Exploit it

Something I was blessed with

Spitting knowledge, given power

Devour, fake individuals and cowards

Like a messenger

Prophet to be

Wisdom gained from experience

My life's a liability

Comfort…ability far from me

Struggle to the light from the darkest peak

With the strongest peeps

Loved the streets

Now I'm in love with the beat

Can't stop writing from the heart my minds asleep

---

[12] C.O.D.E is Ceeza Omega da Exodus. Ceeze or Ceeza was my nickname. Omega is the last letter in the Greek alphabet. I was the youngest one in my closest group of friends. And Exodus meant I was going to bring all my peoples out of the struggle. C.O.D.E is pronounced *co-dee*.

SPEAK WHAT I KNOW AND I KNOW WHAT I SEE

DON'T SEE BIG MONEY

YOU WON'T HEAR ME SAY IT

I SEE THE WORLD FROM THE KNEES OF SOMEBODY PRAYING

KIDS GETTING SLAIN ON A ONE-WAY AVENUE

ALL ABOUT THE REVENUE

DOLLAR BILLS IS CRITICAL

POLITICALLY CORRECT POVERTY IS CATCHING THE DEATHS

BIG NI&&AS OWN THE DEBTS, JUST TO GET A REP'

THAT'S THEY THING

CHANGING THE GAME NOTHING BUT CHANGING NAMES

PREPARE FOR THE WORST

I'M ABOUT DONE

THIS ARTIST WILL RETAIN TO WRITE ONCE IN A LIFETIME A MASTERPIECE

HOOK: ONCE IN A LIFETIME A CLASSIC IS BORN

ONCE IN A LIFETIME A UNIQUE PIECE OF WORK GETS THE CREDIT THAT IT'S WORTH

ONCE IN A LIFETIME A KING SHALL REIGN

ONCE IN A LIFETIME A FORTUNE WILL BRING, ONCE IN A LIFETIME A MASTERPIECE… THAT'S ME C.O.D.E THE BEAST   LET ME SPEAK!

11/19/02

"MY GIRL, MY NI&&AS, MY FAMM"

DAMN BOO WHY YOU

WHY COULDN'T YOU BE THE SECOND LADY THAT I COMMITTED TO

THAT WAY I COULD'VE SPENT THE REST OF MY LIFE WITH YOU

I MISS YOU, I LOVE AND ADORE YOU

I'M SORRY FOR ALL THE PAIN YOU HAD TO GO THROUGH

BECAUSE OF ME, YOU COULDN'T LIVE IN HAPPY MATRIMONY

I TRIED MY BEST

I GUESS

YOU KNOW ME LIKE NO ONE ELSE

YOU TREAT ME LIKE THE KING I WANNA BE

AND I LEFT YOU LIKE AN AVERAGE NI&&A DO

I'M SORRY BOO

I DON'T KNOW WHAT ELSE TO SAY

CAN I MAKE IT UP TO YOU IN ANOTHER WAY

YOU BROUGHT THE SOFTER SIDE OUTTA ME

AND YOU LOVE ME GENUINELY

YOU MY FIRST WIZ THE MOTHER OF MY KID

YOU SHOWED ME WHAT LOVE IS AND HOW LOVE FEEL

I JUST CAUSED YOU HEARTACHE AND PAIN

I'M THE REASON WHY YOU CRIED ON MOST OF THEM DAYS

I WASN'T A HUSBAND JUST AN ACTOR WITH HUSBAND WAYS

YA SOFT FACE

BEAUTIFUL SMILE

YA TENDER TOUCH WHEN YOU TOUCH ME WITH YA BEAUTIFUL STYLE

YOU WILD

THAT'S WHAT I LIKE ABOUT YOU

ADAPTABLE, STRONG-MINDED AND DETERMINED

UNDERSTANDING, LOVING AND CARING

YOU I SHOULD'VE CHERISHED

YOU THE ONE I MARRIED

YOU, ARE, MY, GIRL

HOOK: MY GIRL, MY NI&&AS, MY FAMM

MY WORLD, MY HEART, MY MANS

LOVE, RESPECT, AND LOYALTY,

MY GIRL, MY NI&&AS, MY FAMM

IN A SHORT TIME WE KNOWN EACH OTHER WE BECAME BROTHERS

TOGETHER FOREVER NO MATTER WHATEVA, WHENEVER, WHEREVER

TO INFINITY DOG

YO' FAMM IS MY FAMM

AND THAT'S WHAT I CONSIDER LOVE

LIFE IS TRIFE

BUT US 4 WE GONNA SUCCEED

IF 1 MAKES IT OUT THE HOOD, HE GONNA PULL THE OTHER 3

NOW THAT'S TEAMWORK

WE BLOOD BROTHERS HERE

WE SHARED CRIBS AND CHICKS, MONEY AND WHIPS, AND HUSTLING STRIPS

WE ALL WENT THROUGH SH!T IN OUR LIFE

WHEN WE OPEN OUR EYES, ONE OF US WAS BESIDE OUR SIDE, READY TO RIDE

ON ANY NI&&A F@CKING WIT FAMM

GET DEAD WHERE YOU STAND A HAIR HARMED ON ANY MY MANS

YO I LOVE MY NI&&AS

P', GOTTI AND HARDROC

THEY MY NI&&AS TO MY BODY DROP

6FT. UNDERGROUND TO MY CORPSE GET ROT

I SMOKED A LUNG WITH NI&&AS

DUE TO STRUGGLES IN LIFE

SMOKED THE OTHER LUNG WITH MY NI&&AS

CUZ WE VENT WHEN WE HIGH

YOU KNOW I'M HIGH RIGHT NOW SO LET ME VENT REAL QUICK

YOU MEAN SOMETHING TO ME, INDIVIDUALLY

CUZ ALL YA'LL GOT A PURPOSE

GOTTI YOU THE GROWN YOUNG MAN

OLDER IN AGE, YET YOUNG IN YA WAYS

YOU KEEP ME ON MY TOES IN THE STRUGGLE DAY TO DAY

P', YOU MY OTHER HALF

MY TWIN BUT DARK SKIN

ENEMY TURNED FRIEND, FRIEND TURNED BROTHER AND BROTHER 'TIL END

HARDROC EVEN THOUGH YOU LOCKED

YOU MY NI&&A OCK

GOD-BROTHER FROM BLOOD BROTHER

MY BODYGUARD YO YOU KNOW I LOVE YOU

DAMN

THAT SH!T IS 4REAL

YO I LOVE MY NI&&AS!!!

HOOK

11/21 - 11/22/02

The last four songs (including this song) were written during my first month home after my discharge. I was living with the cousin I worked with before I went to the Marines. It was the same as the last time. All I did was watch porn, get high, write raps, look for jobs and girls, and play video games. Mind you, I had my son with me. What a role model, right?

How Does It End?

The Beginning of the End

I smoked weed (literally) everyday from August 2002 until February 2003, even though I was aware of the consequences with the Marine Corps, with my son, with my job search, and with my life.

In November of 2002 I was discharged from the military for a pattern of misconduct. After my discharge I intended to divorce my wife. I came back to Baltimore with my son, but it lasted less than a month.

By Thanksgiving of 2002 I was missing my wife due to jealousy and the lack of sex. So, I went back to California to supposedly try to work out our marriage.

Christmas 2002 came and I wasn't working, just leeching off of my wife.

January 2003 we were back to wanting a divorce.

The Middle of the End

In February 2003 my wife and I had an argument on base that escalated to the point where I attempted to hurt her again.

"I don't care where you go, but you gotta get up out of here," she said.

I shouted, "What! You know I don't have anywhere to go, and you're still going to kick me out!"

"Yup. I'm tired of the bullsh!t. It's time for me to move on without you," she fired back.

"OK. I got you," was the last thing I said before I lost it. I charged at her with my hands ready to choke the life out of her. As I approached her swift and furiously, she ran out the house screaming, "Don't kill me, don't kill me." She ran right to the neighbor's house and called the military police.

She was right. I honestly believe if my wife would've stayed there in the hallway, I would've choked her. Would I have killed her? I can't say. But I would've choked her as hard as I could, I do believe that.

My son, who was one and a half years old, was also in the house during this rage. As fired up as I was, I had enough sense to send my son out the front door to the same neighbor's house.

Here's a quick backdrop. We were living in the base-housing on the Marine Corps Base in Camp Pendleton, Ca. We were both Marines. However, I had been discharged three months earlier. My wife was still active duty, and I was technically a civilian during this present situation. That fact played into my current mentality. I was not about to go back to jail, by no means.

After I let my son go I grabbed two steak knives, closed all the blinds in the house, and waited for what I thought would be my final battle in life. I was scared, suicidal, and homicidal. I was going to fight the MP's until they killed me, but right as they pulled up to the house panic took over. I put the steak knives back, grabbed the keys to her car and bolted. The MP's were trying to get my attention, but I ran straight to the car, got in, turned the car on, and drove as fast as I could down our extremely tight street taking the police cars passenger side mirrors with me.

I stopped at the main intersection leading out of the housing area we lived in. At this intersection the MP's surrounded my car. They did the whole police thing with guns drawn, telling me to get out, etc, etc. Instead of surrendering, I drove my car right at them thinking they would shoot me, (I was in California), but they didn't. I ended up hitting one officer and smashing two police cars in what eventually became a car chase that shut down the largest Marine base in the U.S. The chase concluded with the police spiking my tires and my attempt to drive into a light pole. I then resisted arrest, was maced, and flipped out while literally screaming and crying for them to "just shoot me".

Since I was a civilian on government property, I was sent to the Federal Metropolitan Correctional Center in San Diego, Ca.

Even though this was my story, that doesn't mean that it *has to be* someone else's story. Looking at it from where I'm sitting now, there was no logical way that I would've made it out of that mess-of-a-life alive; especially to make it out in my right frame of mind with some type of positive future to look forward to. However, the story doesn't end there.

The End...

I hadn't been in jail since I was 17, the week before my high school graduation to be exact. This time I was 22, and on a different coast from my hometown. "WHAT DID I JUST DO" kept scrolling across the forefront of my mind. I swore I'd never go to jail again. I did everything I could to get the MP's to shoot me. Why was I going through this hell? Oh, how I wished life could just end.

I spent the first 48 hours silently and bitterly going through MCC's processing. The following 24 hours would prove to be the nucleus in a future I never thought could exist.

I reached the holding floor of MCC, and from there they sent me to medical. At medical I met an older man.

"What got you here there young man?" The older man asked.

Trying to be discreet, I answered, "Stupidity."

A short time after, I explained to him what happened. Right before I left the medical floor he said, "You know what you need to do."

I looked at him with a blank face and replied, "What is that?"

"Pick up that *book*," he said, as if I was supposed to know what he was talking about.

When I got back to the holding floor, the only book in my cell was a Bible. I picked it up, tried to read it, and put it back down. It wasn't working. At least not fast enough. Later that evening, I got served a restraining order for my wife and son, our house, babysitter, car, and work place. I had no family. I had no friends. I had no one. I was alone in a California federal jail, three thousand miles away from my home and family in Baltimore, Md. Depression sank in heavy like an anchor hitting the bottom of the sea. I went back to my room, got my bathing towel, tied one end to the top bunk, tied the bottom end around my neck, and tried to hang myself. But death continued to elude me.

...and a New Beginning

After attempting suicide again, I was sent to the floor where all the medical cases, older people, and problem people from other floors were housed. Right as I walked through the door, the older man that I met in medical was walking out. He stopped me and told me to go check out the Bible study they were having. I had nothing else better to do, so I went. The lady who led the Bible study was discussing covenants: how God made a covenant with those in the Old Testament, and how God made a covenant with everyone else through His Son Jesus Christ. Of course, I had no idea what she was talking about. Yet, that night was the beginning of a new life to come.

I had two cellmates, one big black guy and one Mexican. I slept on a mattress on the floor, kind of in the corner. That night I was reading a book when the correctional officer locked our cell. I tried to let my mind wander in the pages of the fiction story. But by the time we reached "lights out", my mind wasn't ready to turn off. I kept thinking "WHAT DID I JUST DO". My life was ruined. And just then, what my grandmother had been saying all these years and what that the Bible study lady said about that covenant stuff came back to me. I cried out to the God of the Bible, "I have made a mess of my life. Either You take over, or I'm going to end up in and out of jail and in a grave. I don't know what else to do. Please take over of my life God, or kill me."

Within my first month in jail and my first month being a born-again believer in Jesus Christ (who I was later told more about), Jesus performed His second miracle in my life. (The first miracle was not letting me die those numerous times). Despite being served the restraining order, Jesus brought my wife back. I remember the correctional officers telling me that I had an attorney visit, and when I went out to the visiting room it was my wife. I stood in the visitor's doorway stunned, and cried to the point that the guard had to push me in. She said she only came because my son kept asking about me. Our first visit became the first of many more visits. Jesus had restored my relationship with my wife. He gave me another chance.

A month or so later, my wife was told she had to go to Iraq. We prayed and fasted until her final overseas checkpoint. My wife, for reasons neither we nor the military were able to explain, didn't pass the medical checkpoint. Jesus kept my wife from going to Iraq. He performed another miracle.

During the eight months I spent in MCC, I went through two federal defenders. There were no witnesses for me. It was me against the military police officers involved. I didn't plead out, but I did tell the judge what I was guilty of. The judge said that's not all I was being prosecuted for. So I took it to trial. I was facing 48 to 72 months for assaulting a military police officer with a deadly weapon and intent to cause great bodily harm. I never got on the stand. There was testimony after testimony about what I had done that day. All I had on my side was Jesus. Well, after a couple of hours of deliberation, Jesus was all I needed. I was acquitted of *all* charges! Jesus had performed another miracle.

Even though freedom was so close, it still managed to slip my grasp. I had a bench warrant from the county of Vista, Ca. for assaulting two men with a deadly weapon in 2001. I wasn't being released to freedom. I was being released to go to a San Diego prison facility, and later transferred to Vista county jail. But by this time, my foundation in Jesus was solid. I was awaiting another miracle from my Savior.

The setting seemed familiar. I had a public defender and no witnesses for me. It was me against the county's witnesses, victims, and the arresting detective. Looked like an open and shut case. I even went as far as to plead guilty. I read my note to the judge and left the rest in the hands of Jesus. I spent two months in Vista. The DA couldn't locate the witnesses, victims, or arresting detective. All they had was my confession. Instead of giving me the max sentence for my crime, they gave me time served and three years probation. I was going home. Jesus did it again, another miracle.

In this short span of time I went from an extremely confused, angered, broken man, not truly knowing or caring if there was a God who wanted a relationship with me or not, to knowing from personal and physical experience that God is real and He wants a relationship with me. His name is Jesus Christ, and with Jesus in control of my life *all things are possible!*

The old me:

The new me:

My way of being set free from *the* lifestyle and mentality you've read of (and didn't read of) was and is Jesus Christ. I know what you're thinking, "that's religion, and you don't need or want religion", *and neither do I.*

Religion is not what delivered me from jail and death. Religion is not what set me free from the life I lived and the way I thought. Meeting Jesus and then having a relationship with Him made me realize that He *is* the only One who can make my life what it's supposed to be, victorious and purposeful. Realizing that fact, and then Jesus making Himself real in my life *with evidence*—that is, by delivering me from jail, death, changing my heart, mentality, lifestyle, and revealing to me what He created me for—*is not religion*. It's Love! It's Jesus, the one true God!

Jesus took the "me" you have witnessed through reading this book—and there is more that wasn't presented in this book—and completely changed that "me" to a new person. Religion *can't* do that, ever! Only the real God with *the* power to change a heart and mind can do that, guaranteed every time. He loved me into the person I am presently, by taking the time to make Himself real to me everyday. He was my Way out of my old lifestyle, my old mentality, and (at that time) my definite ending. No job, *especially* one which doesn't offer any future can completely change a person as jacked up (messed up) as I was. Every religion is like a job, something you do regularly that doesn't offer any future. I am not offering you religion. I'm *inviting* you to the Way that paid my debt to God, set me free from the old, changed my life completely, and gave me a new life, purpose, real peace of mind, real happiness, security, and hope. If He did it for a jacked up person like me, and is still doing for me now, He can do the same things for you but only if you believe and accept Him as your Savoir and Lord. You have to be on His team to receive His benefits.

FINAL WORDS

Do you feel like life has dealt you a bad hand? Maybe you've grown up or had to live in an environment that is plagued with negativity, with nothing to offer, and with nothing to be gained. Maybe you've been victimized or abused. Maybe you were born in or have fallen into poverty and it seems like there's no hope of coming out. Maybe you're confused about who you are and/or why you're here. Maybe you're well-off and you think you have everything you need or want, yet you still feel empty—something is missing or incomplete. Maybe you're content with your life, everything is good no complaints; but because life *will* throw the *unexpected* you can't say your life will stay that way.

There is only One answer to *all* of life's problems. There's only One who promises new life, and to reveal who you are and why you were created. There is only One who will make you whole, give your life security, inner peace, purpose, etc. And, this One has *proved* it for 2,000 years (still counting) and through the billions of changed lives of those just like you and I. Yes He can do it, if you give Him the chance to take control and let Him do it His way.

Be careful and be aware. This world presents the things that are bad or harmful as normal and the things that are good or up building as different or weird. The bad/negative is looked upon as good or ok, but the good/positive is frowned upon as if it were bad or negative. Music, TV, movies, celebrities, and athletes are the main sources influencing today's trends, and trends influence people's lifestyles. If you get a large enough amount of similar lifestyles, you get what's shaping today's society. So let's be real, who's really running your life, you or the influences?

Now knowing this information, "who you with", a lifestyle or a trend that promotes sex, promiscuity, drugs, alcohol, violence, and anything else that *will* cause you long term harm (whatever that may be)? Many people see these things as fun or needed to have fun, and/or as something to make you feel comfortable about your place among your peers. Trust me, I lived it, for over 12 years. It's no where near as fun in the end as it *appears* to be in the beginning.

Why not be with the One who loves you so much that He gave His life to pay the punishment you deserve for your sins (lying, cheating, lusting, hate, stealing, idolizing, ungodly thoughts, ungodly words, etc)? The One who has a purpose not to harm your life, but rather for you to be something great with the gifts He's given you. This is the One who promises and guarantees that you'll be with Him forever, but only if you believe in Him. He will not offer this temporary artificial pleasure here, which only last for a short time and causes more problems and drama than you already had. Instead, He promises a fulfilling, worthwhile, adventurous life *here*, and eternal "for real" pleasure with Him when you die. Or, you can continue on earth, and then the real hell in Hell!

"WHO YOU WITH?"

I ask you, please don't judge Jesus based on His messy, imperfect followers. Let Him speak for Himself by what He does in your own life. How many of us can relate to being knocked (criticized, belittled, rejected) up front without a chance, or being knocked based off our parents, friends, or whatever else but not us? Hey, I met Jesus in jail in Cali when I was 22. Jesus will meet you wherever and whenever you call on Him to be saved. He turned my last two jail experiences from confinement to true freedom, education, and lasting memories.

Whoever said Jesus is boring has obviously never read His Story, the Bible. *Religion is what's boring*. And even though certain churches may be boring to you, the Creator of all things is not boring!

Jesus had large crowds everywhere He went. There's a passage in the Bible where it says, there was noise (commotion) when Jesus was in the house (Mark 2:1-2). Jesus was into getting people pumped (motivated), but for the right things not the wrong things. Therefore, He being God knows exactly how to keep you interested and get you pumped for life. In fact, that's what Jesus said He came here to do. He came to give you life and life more fulfilling, interesting, hopeful, bearable, purposeful, and to achieve the impossible.

That's the God I believe, serve, and live for. I don't know the Jesus you're thinking about, but it's obviously not the Jesus I believe in, nor the one described in His Bible. Forget what others say, Jesus is not religion. Jesus wants a _personal relationship_ with you, so He can truly show _you_ who He is as described in His Bible. Come on, He's the only Man that has turned the world upside down for more than 2,000 years and still counting! He's the only Man that has dramatically and radically changed the lives of billions of people's for over 2,000 years! Who else has a longer _running_ record? Actually, no one else is even close to His record! Tell me again, who "ain't" real!

Listen, not all of His family is boring, stuck-up, messy, or hypo-critical, maybe dysfunctional, but what family isn't. Some of us have tapped into who He truly is and what He truly has for our lives. That's why we live like we do: different from the norm, sincere, and living an interesting life, _all for_ Him. Again, please don't judge Jesus based on His inconsistent "Christians", give _Him_ a chance to speak for Himself by what He does in your own life.

The life I live, I live for the One who gave His life for me. There's no other way I can show Jesus how thankful I am for all He's done for me except by living (of course with His help) in a way that displays my gratitude and respect. He has not and will never let me down, nor make me regret living for Him. He has lived up to everything the Bible says He is and can do. I know I'm not special. If He can do it for a jacked up, former [13]thugged out, pothead, drug dealer, sex addict, abuser, abused, selfish, liar, prideful, crazy knucklehead like me, then He can do it for anybody.

Jesus says, "I stand at the door and knock" (Revelation 3:20). What are you going to do? Either let Him in, or turn Him away. You have to make a choice: the One who loves you and died for your sins, or the life that offers you temporary artificial pleasure but always ends in emptiness.

Life (what you do and how you live) is the reality of choices. You can do absolutely nothing without first making a choice to do it. Therefore, your tomorrow is the consequence of your choices today. _Today_ is the

---

[13] "Thugged out" meaning brutal, violent, and crazy acting.

day. There may not be a tomorrow to make another choice. *Today* I lay before you life and death. Whoever or whatever you choose *is* who or what you will serve.

"WHO YOU WITH?"

Not What You Think

It's Not What You Think...

The Christian movement is *not* about acting like, being, or claiming to be perfect, condemning people, or calling them out (although some Christians do this); but rather it's about loving people just as Jesus loves us—through forgiveness, acceptance, encouragement, development, deliverance, and restoration.

It's Not What You Think...

The Christian movement is *not* about teaching, restricting, or maintaining rules, rituals, and ceremonies in order to receive something; that's religion. The Christian movement is *not* about seeking after one particular thing or things; but rather believing in Jesus means you have found "that" which fills the empty space the soul is desiring to fill—a relationship with its Creator.

It's Not What You Think...

The Bible is *not* a rule book, but rather the roadmap of life. The Bible is *not* just a book of things to do, or contradictions, or a good book written by man. It is one story from beginning (Genesis) to the end (Revelation) about God and creation. It's told by God Himself who used 40 different people (just like we use pencils/pens to record what we want to record) as instruments to record His story as a source for us to know who He truly is, the beginning of life, how we are to live and function on earth, and the ending of life.

It's Not What You Think...

The church is *not* a building that houses religion or religious people and activities (although some Christians treat it that way); but rather the church is a place of fellowship, education, healing, and service for all who belong to and love Jesus, as well as all those who need or want help, and/or want to get to know Jesus.

It's Not What You Think…

Believing in Jesus is *not* a religion, but rather a personal relationship with the One who created you and loves you enough to die for your sins. Believing in Jesus is *not* about doing a list of things so you can go to Heaven or to receive anything else; but rather you live your life for Jesus out of gratitude and respect because of who He is, what He's done for you, is doing for you, and going to do for you.

It's Not What You Think…

Jesus Christ is *not* just a good person, or just a prophet, or a fake; but rather Jesus Christ is real, relevant, saving, and changing millions and millions of people's lives for 2,000 years and counting. This Jesus Christ is *not* found in Jehovah's Witness, Mormons, Christian Science, or anything else; but the real Jesus Christ is found only in the Holy Bible and in the real Christian movement.

It's Not What You Think…

Jesus was *not* sent for Himself; but rather Jesus came to earth to die and resurrect for lost people, so that [1]those who believe in Him are guaranteed life on earth with purpose, power, inner joy and peace, and hope; [2]those who believe in Him are guaranteed that He'll take care of all their needs; [3]those who believe in Him are guaranteed that no matter how bad life may be (because life will bring bad days), it will always work out for their good; and [4]those who believe in Him are guaranteed that when they die they'll spend eternity with Him. No religion, nor any other belief offers you guarantees, then provides over billions of lives and over 2,000 years of fulfilling its guarantees! No one nor anything else but Jesus can and has performed this. Come, witness it for yourself.

Do You Know?

Do You Know?

There is Good News and there is bad news. In order for the good news to be good I have to share the bad news first. The bad news is because everybody has broken God's law (sinned/disobeyed God in your heart, thoughts, and action), God requires a consequence/penalty to be paid (just like if you break the law you have to suffer the consequence—do the crime do the time/or pay the fine), and the penalty for sin is eternal separation from God and eternal punishment (eternal prison).

Do You Know?

No matter how big or small the sin is, no matter how much or how less you've sinned, (and you'll sin again), one sin against God still requires the same penalty as many sins. In other words, you are a sinner and you are doomed to eternal prison because God is holy and just and He has to judge sin; much like a judge has to sentence a felony crime.

Do You Know?

The Good News is Jesus—and nobody else but Jesus—loves **you** so much that *He died* the worst death possible *to pay for the consequence of your sins by taking the punishment from God that you deserve*. This means through Jesus **you** are guaranteed forgiveness from God for **your** sins past, present and future.

Do You Know?

Only Jesus Christ offers to rescue **you** from the eternal consequence of sin as a gift. He loves **you** and that's why He died for **you**. No religion, nor any other belief can say that their "god" did that for them! Nor can any religion or other belief say that their "god" resurrected to prove and guarantee their salvation. Only Jesus died and resurrected to prove His power to save. Jesus is inviting **you** to be a part of His family, and receive all that He has for **you**.

Will You Accept His Invitation?

Do You Know?

If you don't believe in Jesus Christ you'll miss out on an *awesome* relationship with the Creator of this beautiful, detailed, massive Universe. And, due to mankind being full of sin, you'll spend eternity in the place with everyone else who rejected His gift and still has to pay the penalty of their sin, and that place is Hell (eternal prison).

<u>So what are you going to do now, accept or reject?</u>
<u>Just remember, your life is on the line.</u>

Do You Know?

For those who are skeptical, what happens if it is real? What happens if when you die afterwards your eyes are suddenly opened to see the face of Jesus? What happens when He says you're condemned because of your sin? What happens when He sentences you to eternal punishment—Hell? Why risk your eternity on what could be faulty understanding and the chance that Jesus isn't God and the only Way for salvation? I'm not trying to scare you to believe, simply speaking His reality. If you don't believe in Jesus Christ and your skepticism is false, you just lost everything. I used to be skeptical too. And just so you'll know, there is logical reasoning and solid evidence to why believing in Jesus Christ is true. It's not blind faith, faith simply brings it all together.

Why Not

Why won't you believe in Jesus?

Is it because you simply don't believe in God? I see, you'll believe in Darwin's theory of evolution that scientists have found to be flawed. Or, you can believe the reason our planet is not colliding into other things floating in space is because we're floating on an invisible axis. Yet, you won't believe there's a God even though you see and know how detailed our planet is as well as the other things floating in space; plus the fact that science has yet to find concrete evidence to disprove a Supreme Being, but more to approve it.

Why won't you believe in Jesus?

Is it because you don't want to believe in a God that allows so much pain and chaos? That's not God's fault. We are the sinners, we do the sins. And so we choose to be self-centered, prideful, kill, enslave, destroy, rape, condemn, restrict, discriminate, accumulate, exploit, etc. God, in spite of all this mess we make, provides a way for us to find peace, joy, love, acceptance, rest, freedom, opportunity, forgiveness, equality, etc, through the sacrifice that Jesus Christ made when He died for our sins. This is how He shows His love in spite of the pain and chaos.

Why won't you believe in Jesus?

Is it because it's hard for you to believe that Jesus is who He said He is? Well, how do you know anybody is who they actually say they are? You take their word for it and in time you see if it proves to be true. That's the same with Jesus. The billions of people who have taken Jesus at His word, their lives have been dramatically changed and this itself proves Him to be who He said He is. That's not including the other solid evidence that is there if one really wants to know.

Why won't you believe in Jesus?

Is it because of what the critics say? Do you believe the critics when they lie about you, even when they say they have so-called "proof"? So, why would you believe the Jesus critics without finding out for yourself? You wouldn't want people to claim you to be a liar, a fake, etc, without giving you a chance to prove yourself. Why hold Jesus to the same criticism without giving Him a chance to prove Himself? If He can truly change the hearts and the lives of the worst of the worst, the needy of the needy, and the hurt of the hurt in life—I'm living proof and I know many others—to the point where their living for Him, representing Him, and introducing others to Him; that's something worth giving a chance and taking an honest look at.

Why won't you believe in Jesus?

Is it because you don't want to be a part of a bunch of hypocrites? I hate to say it, but everyone is hypocritical in some fashion. You'd be denying yourself, family, and friends by saying you don't want to be a part of a bunch of hypocrites, because we all make mistakes. You'd live a lonely, miserable life. You would be amazed at how a lot of believers actually aren't as hypocritical as you think; if you took the time to stop judging them like you want them to stop judging you.

Why won't you believe in Jesus?

Is it because you don't want to get involved with religion? Again, Jesus doesn't like religion either. Actually, Jesus condemned the people who overly stressed religion. Jesus is about relationships, not religion. And so, believing in Jesus is having a personal relationship with Jesus (like marriage, not a job like religion); and in that relationship you're showing Jesus, through your obedience, your thanks for Him "taking the bullet" for you.

Why won't you believe in Jesus?

Is it because you believe there are also "other ways" to God? Well, none of the "other ways" provide your salvation by a sincere confession of belief. In those "other ways" *you* have to *work for* your salvation. None of the "other ways" provide a guarantee for your salvation or whatever else they claim. Only Jesus does. So why risk your eternity and take the chance that Jesus is *not* the only way, just to go to Hell if He really is?

If you will accept His invitation, then repeat this prayer:

Father God I confess that I am a sinner and in need of Your forgiveness. I believe that Jesus Christ died for my sins and rose from the dead. I accept Jesus Christ as my personal Savior and Lord. By Your grace, *I willingly turn away from my life of sin*. Jesus, *help me to live* a life pleasing to You. In Your name I pray, Amen.

If you've prayed this prayer, congratulations, you're now a part of Jesus' family! Yes we are dysfunctional, but what family isn't. That just shows you that we're still human and no where near perfect. We've just been forgiven and giving a new chance *to live our life for* Jesus.

As a child of God you need to *get a Bible*. Read it to learn about God (Jesus). Follow the instructions in it, for the Bible is God's roadmap for our life. *Talk to God* all day about everything. *He'll listen and direct you* toward your future. Without communication, how will you ever know *what* you are to do and *where* you're supposed to go? Last but not least, join a church (a genuine group of Christians, <u>not</u> Jehovah Witness or Mormons) and be baptized. It's good to *surround yourself with other believers who can help you* in your new life. Again, congratulations, and I'll see you around either here or in eternity.

If you refuse to accept His invitation, then you have just turned down ***the greatest love*** and the most priceless and valuable free gift...***your salvation***.

Whether you believe it or not, I truly was skeptical of "this" at one time. But the more I reflected on a God loving me so much that He came to earth to die for my sins so I won't have to suffer the penalty/punishment I deserve but have a relationship with Him, the more I realized why would I believe and live for anyone/anything else.

Know this, I shared all of my personal business with you to help. Jesus Christ rescued me and gave me a new life. He can rescue and give you a new life too. Remember, if He can change a jacked up me and work wonders in my life, He can do it for you and anybody else. He loves you and wants to be a part of your life. Please trust me, accept His invitation. It'll be the best decision you'll ever make, guaranteed. I'm an email away if you ever need to talk.

Did You Enjoy The Book?

If you enjoyed this book, your feedback and questions are welcomed and encouraged.

Send all comments, questions, and requests to: CBDAVIS80@GMAIL.COM

For more info on the author and his other works:
www.biblicallyshaped.com

Ceeze exits…

www.ingramcontent.com/pod-product-compliance
Lightning Source LLC
Chambersburg PA
CBHW020258290526
45784CB00003B/1293